BROADWAY

In the beginning BROADWAY had two small streams that flowed down the hill on either side of what is now the High Street. Houses were built on the outer banks and down the middle the track developed into the wide and curving main street from which the village takes its name. The streams were piped in 1862, dip holes being left at regular intervals for buckets. About this time the flow of water diminished due to tapping at the source springs. The streams were finally put under ground in about 1900.

In the old days before the introduction of tarmac, the roads were made of crushed Cotswold stone and known as the 'yellow roads'. In the winter they were kept free of mud, which was dragged to the side with scrapers and allowed to pile up. In the summer this seeded and the green verges gradually grew. Old photographs make it clear that before 1892, no trees lined the roadsides.

The Green itself has been the centre of the village since the earliest days. In 1251 the Abbots of Pershore were granted a weekly market on Tuesday and a fair lasting three days at Whitsun. At the market young men and women used to come and offer themselves for hire, standing by a market cross which stood at the corner of The Green. This cross remained until nearly 1900 when it was taken down and used to prop up a barn. Older records show that in 1351 such rough sports as bear and badger baiting took place on The Green and for centuries the annual fair was a major event.

A BRIEF HISTORY
Broadway in the County of Worcestershire

We know that there have been settlements of people from the earliest times in the region of Broadway Green, from the discovery of pottery dating back to the ancient Beaker people of 1900BC and Roman times. But the Broadway we know today was established after the Battle of Dyrham in 577AD when a group of the South Saxons called the Hi-Wicci defeated the local tribes and advanced up the Severn Valley as far as Worcester, conquering most of Gloucestershire and Worcestershire.

With the coming of Christianity and the building of the monasteries, it seems that at a very early date Broadway became a possession of the Benedictine Abbey of Pershore. A fact which was recorded by a Charter granted by King Edgar in 972. Broadway remained a possession of the Abbot of Pershore for the next 560 years, until King Henry VIII's Reformation of 1538 when it passed to the Crown (24 January 1539). Until this time it had supplied one quarter of the Abbey's income.

Broadway, like many of its neighbouring villages, prospered in the wake of the Dissolution and its position at the foot of the Cotswold escarpment where the great track-way between South Wales and London left the Severn plain and made it a place of considerable importance.

The Crown sold the Manor of Broadway in 1558 and for the next 200 years it was owned by a series of interesting people. First and perhaps least known, was Sir William Babington who was forced to sell in 1575 to meet expenses when his son Antony became involved as principal conspirator in the unsuccessful plot to assassinate Queen Elizabeth and free Mary, Queen of Scots from Fotheringay Castle. Antony Babington was hanged, drawn and quartered for his part in the affair.

For the next hundred years it was the turn of the Dastons and Savages, and the Sheldons, their close relations. Ann Sheldon married Francis Savage of Elmley Castle and on his death, she married Antony Daston. It was her sons of Savage parentage who were to inherit her Broadway estates and keep them in that family for 200 years. Ann, known as Mistress Ann, lived at Broadway Court and had the reputation of being 'the most bountiful woman of her degree in all England'.

The Sheldons were some of the largest landowners in the Midlands and it was Ralf Sheldon, Mistress Ann's brother, who bought the remainder of the Manor in 1575, and along with its lands, the Manorial rights. It was this Ralf, who with his father, made the famous Sheldon Tapestries. Sheldons remained in Broadway until 1675 when the Winningtons took over and owned the Manorial rights until as recently as 1947.

The importance of Broadway increased when in about 1600, the stage coach became the accepted mode of travel and Broadway became a major coaching centre. Before the escarpment was climbed, fresh horses had to be found and extra ones too. In all, besides the wagon trains for heavy merchandise as well as numerous traps and private carriages, seven coaches passed daily through Broadway between London, Worcester and beyond.

To serve all this traffic, a large following of grooms, ostlers and blacksmiths grew up in the village. Inns, such as the Lygon Arms, flourished and there were at one time 33 public houses in Broadway. Then suddenly in 1856, the railways came, bringing the coaching days almost to an end.

The traffic stopped and, cut off from the outside world, the village became the haven of beauty, peace and quiet that so attracted the Victorian writers and artists a few decades later.

Ralf Sheldon 1623-1684.

Buildings and places featured in this edition

Russell House

STATION ROAD

PAGE 5 VIEW

Lifford Memorial Hall

The Swan Hotel

Car Park

Burrow's Shop

Brown's Bakery

Sands Farm & Low Farm

Mr Foss's Shop

The Lygon Arms

BACK LA

Farnham House

The Green

COVER VIEW

Cross

HIGH STREET

B 463

PAGE 1 VIEW

Abbot's Grange

Old Post Office

Old Curiosity Shop

Old Ken Shop

Broadway Hotel

Crown & Trumpet

Kylsant House

CHURCH CLOSE

CHURCH STREET

WC Car Park

St Michael's Church

Austin House

SNOWSHILL ROAD

St Eadburgha's Church and The Court - 3/4 mile

Bow Gr

During the second half of the twentieth century, the western world was astir and everywhere men were in revolt against the dirt and squalor brought about by the Industrial Revolution. Artists of the stature of Sir Edward Byrne-Jones, Holman Hunt and Sir John Millais were seeking a new and fresh approach to painting, calling themselves the Pre-Raphaelite Brotherhood. Lord Tennyson was writing poetry the ordinary man could understand. William Morris, socialist-dreamer, poet and painter, was proclaiming the virtues of craftsmanship. From America two artists, Edwin Austin Abbey and Frank Millet, were looking for the ideal of the perfect English village.

The arrival of the railways and the bicycle enabled artists to travel widely and exploring the Cotswolds became a popular pastime. One summer's afternoon two of them, probably Sir Alfred Parsons (painter, botanist and landscape gardener) and Leonard Hutton (author), called on William Morris who was staying at Broadway Tower. It was he who suggested that after tea they should walk down to the village below. In those days there was no tarmac or kerbstones. Along the curving yellow Cotswold stone road, flanked by charming cottages, magnificent farmhouses and one great inn – they knew they had found the beauty, peace and tranquillity they so desired.

Leonard Hutton told Edwin Abbey and Frank Millet of his discovery. They leased Farnham House on Broadway Green and the whole artistic world seems to have followed them there. Alfred Parsons, Henry James, Sir John Hare, Sir John Sargent, Mary Anderson de Navarro, all came to Broadway and made it the most famous village in England. Those lovely golden days continued until the motor car came and spoilt it all.

As an American magazine once put it: 'Nowhere can the ideal of Old England be found in such a perfect state of preservation or so untouched by modern improvements as Broadway. There is scarcely a house which hasn't been painted by a famous artist, there isn't a chimney or doorway which hasn't been sketched.'

Happily, even if its peace has suffered the inevitable disturbance of the motorcar age, Broadway still presents to the world the same beautiful face that so many have drawn and painted.

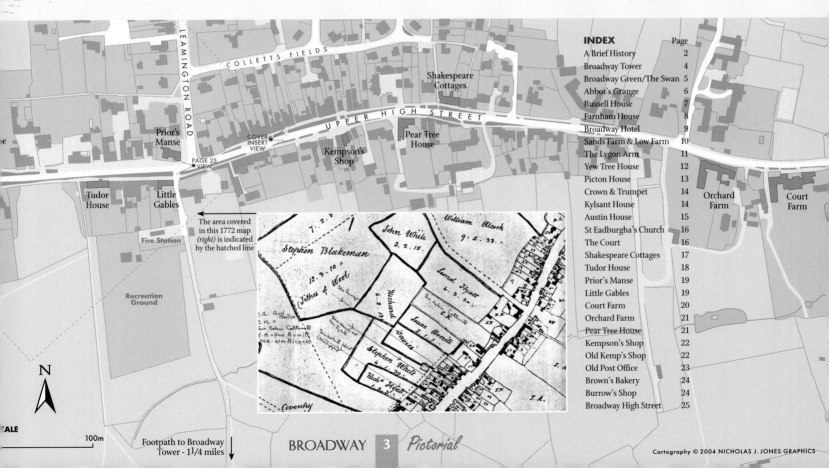

The area covered in this 1772 map (right) is indicated by the hatched line

100m

Footpath to Broadway Tower - 1¼ miles

Cartography © 2004 NICHOLAS J. JONES GRAPHICS

BROADWAY TOWER
Beacon Hill

Turris Lati... ...insis 1854.
MIDDLE HILL.

BROADWAY TOWER stands on Beacon Hill, a landmark overlooking the Vale of Evesham from which thirteen counties can be seen. The Tower was built by Peggy, Countess of Coventry, wife of the 6th Earl, who owned the neighbouring estate of Springhill. Plans dating from 1794, reveal that the architect was the famous James Wyatt.

Some doubt exists as to why the Tower was built. Some would say that it was a signalling tower between Springhill and Croom, Coventry's main estate near Pershore, which is within sight of the Tower.

Broadway Tower today (main photo), with visitors circa 1900 (left) and in 1948 (middle right).
Top left: The stamp used by Thomas Phillipps Press.
Top right: Preparing the beacon fire.
Right: Going up Fish Hill by cart in 1907.

Others claim that it was built simply as a folly. But there is another interesting fact. It is known that during 1797 a great bonfire was lit and fireworks let off by Thomas, Lord Coventry's son. The Tower was constructed the following year, suggesting that it may have been built to celebrate the centenary of the Earldom created in 1697.

In 1827 the Tower was sold to Sir Thomas Phillipps who used it to house his printing press. When he moved to Cheltenham he leased it to two Oxford tutors, Carmen Price and Stone. Price had the Tower renovated in 1867 and encouraged his friends and students to stay there. Among them were Sir Edward Byrne-Jones and William Morris.

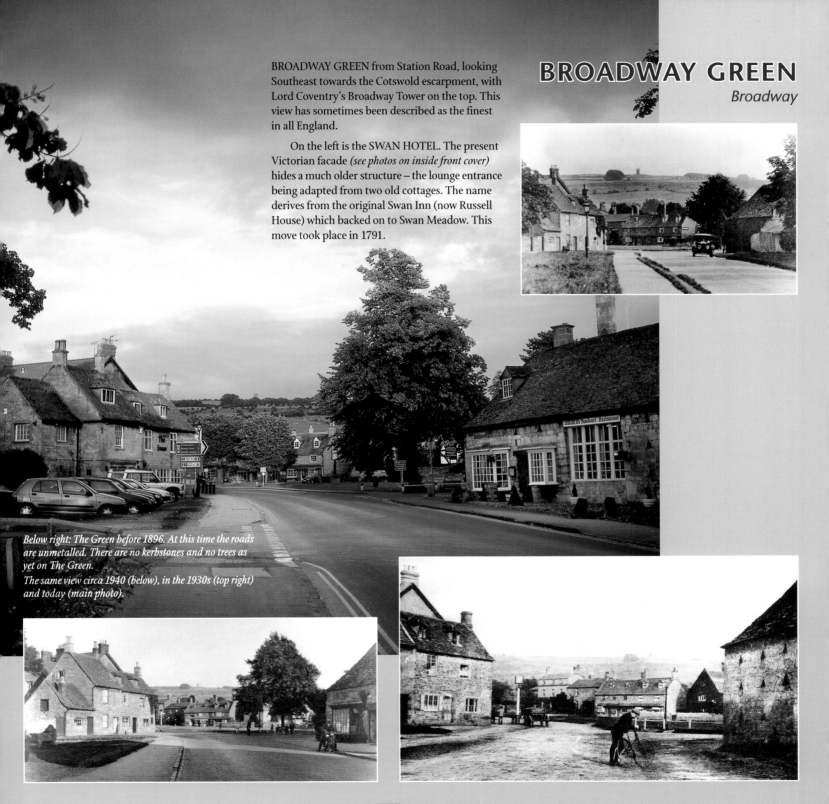

BROADWAY GREEN from Station Road, looking Southeast towards the Cotswold escarpment, with Lord Coventry's Broadway Tower on the top. This view has sometimes been described as the finest in all England.

On the left is the SWAN HOTEL. The present Victorian facade *(see photos on inside front cover)* hides a much older structure – the lounge entrance being adapted from two old cottages. The name derives from the original Swan Inn (now Russell House) which backed on to Swan Meadow. This move took place in 1791.

Below right: The Green before 1896. At this time the roads are unmetalled. There are no kerbstones and no trees as yet on The Green.
The same view circa 1940 (below), in the 1930s (top right) and today (main photo).

ABBOT'S GRANGE
The Green

ABBOT'S GRANGE lies hidden behind the yew hedge facing The Green. It is one of the oldest domestic buildings in Worcestershire, built about 1320 by William de Harvington, Abbot of Pershore, as his summer residence. Until 1900 there was no hedge, the Grange stood open for all to see. Now you can only get a glimpse of it from the drive where you will see its church-like windows.

It is a splendid house built on the lines of an Oxbridge college with a great hall, buttery and oratory. For years it had been in a ruinous condition, having been used as a lock-up and as a house for the poor. In 1896 it was purchased and restored by Frank Millet, the American artist, who lived at Russell House and used Abbot's Grange as a studio. Here painting his famous picture 'Between Two Fires'.

Main picture: Abbot's Grange in 2004.
Above: A early watercolour of Abbot's Grange.
Left: The front of Abbot's Grange about 1890–1900.
Below: The rear of Abbot's Grange after Frank Millet's restoration (right) and in about 1935 (left).

RUSSELL HOUSE
Station Road

RUSSELL HOUSE is situated in the curve of the road from Evesham as it enters the village. Like several houses in the village it takes its name from the family who built it. This house was built by John Russell in 1791 and replaced an old inn named The Swan, so called from the Swan Meadow behind.

In 1886 Frank Millet made this house his home. Initially he leased the property, purchasing it in 1896. He lived there until his death in the Titanic disaster in 1912. The adjoining barn was converted into a large drawing room and studio and you can still see how various doorways have been filled in to achieve this. The elegant porch and gateway are also worth a special look.

Frank Millet, 1860-1912.

Main photo: Russell House as it is today.
Above right: Russell House about 1877. Spot the penny-farthing bicycle being held by the man on the right.
Left: Russell House porch in its original position.
Lower left: Russell House in a dilapidated condition, 1956.
Below: The North Cotswold Hunt meet outside Russell House in 1896.

FARNHAM HOUSE
The Green

FARNHAM HOUSE stands on the corner of The Green and was once the home of the Lord of the Manor. Built about 1660, it demonstrates Cotswold architecture very well, with tall diagonal chimneys, steep gables with dormer windows and little round attic windows; the main windows mullioned with dripmoulds and a string course between the storeys.

Edwin Austin Abbey, pencil sketch by John Singer Sargent.

Main photo: Farnham House today.
Top left: Farnham House, circa 1890.
Middle left: The Pemberton family at the front of Farnham House in 1890. Note the original doorway.
Farnham House and part of The Green in 1896 (left), and shown on a postcard, circa 1920 (right).

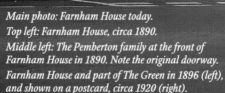

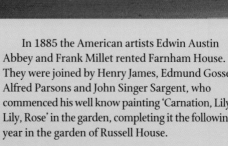

In 1885 the American artists Edwin Austin Abbey and Frank Millet rented Farnham House. They were joined by Henry James, Edmund Gosse, Alfred Parsons and John Singer Sargent, who commenced his well know painting 'Carnation, Lily, Lily, Rose' in the garden, completing it the following year in the garden of Russell House.

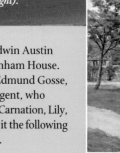

The BROADWAY HOTEL is a half stone and half timber frame building. On an inside door is the date 1575. Over the centuries it has varied in appearance and use. In 1772 it looked much as it does today, but in front of the timbered part stood a small blacksmith's forge abutting on to The Green.

In the next century it became re-wrapped in ivy and was therefore called Ivy House, and was used as a bakehouse owned by Mr Holcroft, the village baker. Colin Houghton's old groom, Arthur Johnson, remembers working there as a baker's lad when the big timbered room (now the hotel lounge) was the baking room, whilst the Holcroft's themselves lived in the stone-built half on the left. In 1930 it became a hotel.

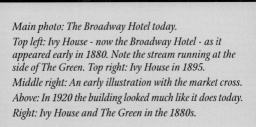

Main photo: The Broadway Hotel today.
Top left: Ivy House - now the Broadway Hotel - as it appeared early in 1880. Note the stream running at the side of The Green. Top right: Ivy House in 1895.
Middle right: An early illustration with the market cross.
Above: In 1920 the building looked much like it does today.
Right: Ivy House and The Green in the 1880s.

SANDS FARM & LOW FARM
The Green

SANDS FARM and LOW FARM until recently formed the offices and showrooms of Gordon Russell Limited - famous for making furniture of the finest quality.

Originally two farmhouses, the lower building (with the two storied porch) bears the date on its chimney 1588. Until 1728 this was the homestead of the Dickens family and known as Dickens House. After the Enclosures Act of 1772, the building became known as Sands Farm taking its name from the common fields behind it.

Main photo: The former headquarters of Gordon Russell Limited, previously Sands Farm and Low Farm in 2003.
Top left: Mrs Julia Bunn owner of Low farm, 1892-1920.
Sands Farm and Low Farm in 1914 (middle left) and in the 1940s (above).
Bottom left: Sands Farm in 1892.

Its front in no way corresponds to the date on the chimney and would seem to have been rebuilt about 1790. By 1916 it had become very rundown and was restored with the two storied porch added. The upper part of Gordon Russell's offices used to be called The Low Farm as its land lay in the lower part of the village near the station.

The passage alongside the chemist shop was blocked by Gordon Russell's showrooms. Until 1916 this was the entrance into the farmyard which had a magnificent thatched barn which was destroyed by incendiary bombs during the war. The passage was re-opened in 2004 and leads into The Russell's development.

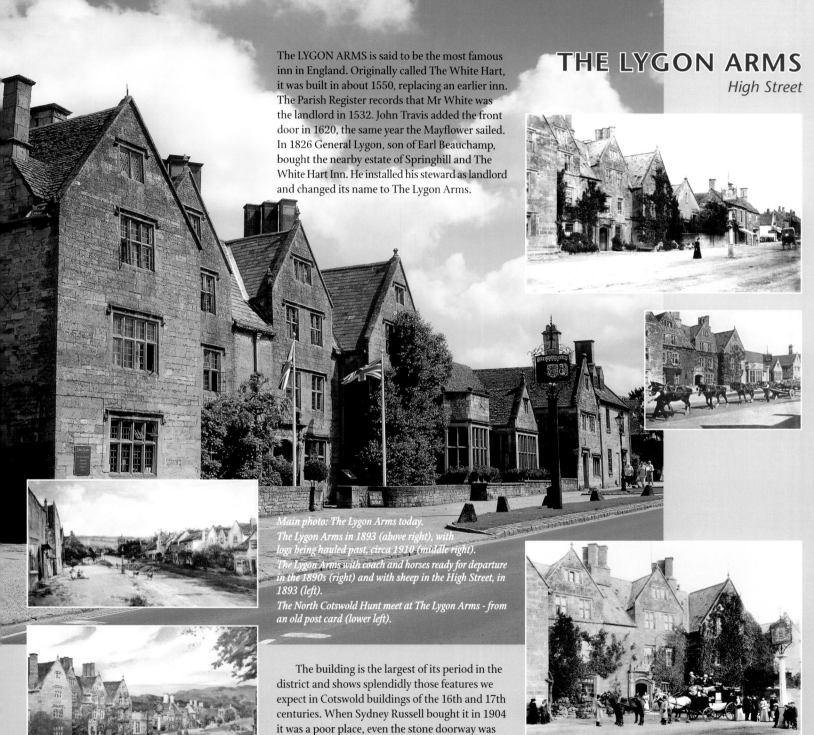

The LYGON ARMS is said to be the most famous inn in England. Originally called The White Hart, it was built in about 1550, replacing an earlier inn. The Parish Register records that Mr White was the landlord in 1532. John Travis added the front door in 1620, the same year the Mayflower sailed. In 1826 General Lygon, son of Earl Beauchamp, bought the nearby estate of Springhill and The White Hart Inn. He installed his steward as landlord and changed its name to The Lygon Arms.

Main photo: The Lygon Arms today.
The Lygon Arms in 1893 (above right), with logs being hauled past, circa 1910 (middle right).
The Lygon Arms with coach and horses ready for departure in the 1890s (right) and with sheep in the High Street, in 1893 (left).
The North Cotswold Hunt meet at The Lygon Arms - from an old post card (lower left).

The building is the largest of its period in the district and shows splendidly those features we expect in Cotswold buildings of the 16th and 17th centuries. When Sydney Russell bought it in 1904 it was a poor place, even the stone doorway was covered with dark brown paint. Mr Russell changed all this and made it the fine hotel you see today.

YEW TREE HOUSE
High Street

YEW TREE HOUSE is a charming early Cotswold house with fine old timber work inside. Originally two dwellings, the upper or eastern part of the property is the oldest, showing all the attributes of a 16th century Cotswold house. The lower part was built about 1750 at the same time that Picton House next door was extended to form the Bell Inn. The Yew tree presents a real problem to clip and to keep alive. The Broadway Trust considers it to be a very important architectural feature and has spent considerable sums trying to preserve it.

Of Yew Tree House, Richard Hagen's comment is: "The end of a series of fine examples of English domestic architecture. The tree itself is a fitting finish and its shape recalls the adjoining gables".

Main photo: Yew Tree House today.
Yew Tree House in 1933 (top left) and in circa 1915 (left).
Right: The VE Parade passes Yew Tree House in 1945. The little boy with the drum, is the author's son Michael.

PICTON HOUSE is the most dignified example of English Renaissance architecture in Broadway. Through the centuries it has played many parts. Built in about 1700 for the Stretch family as a private house, it became a coaching inn named The Bell in 1744. Later it became a school, but about 1830 it was bought by Sir Thomas Phillipps who lived at Middle Hill. Sir Thomas claimed descent from the Phillipps of Piston Castle in Pembrokeshire and therefore named this house Piston House. The gate posts are said to have come from Broadway Court which was demolished in 1773.

The house was originally flanked by the two inner chimneys. The ground floor consisted of the front door, with a pair of windows on each side. It was probably extended and had the archway added when it became an inn.

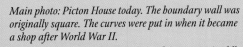

Main photo: Picton House today. The boundary wall was originally square. The curves were put in when it became a shop after World War II.

Picton House in the early 1900s (top right), in 1920 (middle right), in the 1930s (right) and in the 1970s (left).

CROWN & TRUMPET
Church Street

THE CROWN AND TRUMPET (pictured above in 1906) has been an inn for some 150 years and before that was probably a farm. The remains of a drip mould indicate that it originally had mullioned windows and used to be a 17th century Cotswold style house. Kylsant House and St Michael's Church lie beyond.

KYLSANT HOUSE
Church Street

KYLSANT HOUSE in circa 1900 (above), once the home of the Sir Thomas Phillipps, and as it is today (right). Charles McNeill, Master of the North Cotswold Fox Hounds (insert), lived at Kylsant House, 1904.

AUSTIN HOUSE was named after its first owner and built about 1700. It has been greatly enlarged over the years. It is a fine example of the Queen Anne or early Georgian period and is in many ways quite different from the seventeenth century architecture prevalent in Broadway. Lord Lifford, much loved in Broadway, lived here until 1913 and his widow until 1928.

Main photo: Austin House today.
Austin House depicted on a postcard circa 1910 (top right), in the 1950s (right and middle right), note the Elm trees in the foreground field have all since gone.
Below: Lord Lifford in the garden of Austin House in 1899.

The huge yew hedge in the garden was used to hide a five seater 'privy'. The railings in front of the house were the only ones in the village not to be taken down in World War II, as they were said to be contemporary with the house and of importance.

Austin House was the home of the author from 1949, until he moved into the stable wing in 1990.

ST EADBURGHA'S CHURCH
Snowshill Road

ST EADBURGHA'S CHURCH (right) is a fine example of Early English architecture dating from about 1200. Above: A watercolour of St Eadburgha's Church and The Court by Violet Lindsell.

THE COURT
Snowshill Road

THE COURT (in 1890 above), once formed the gate house and entrance to the stables of Broadway Court which stood in the field opposite until its demolition in 1773. Mr and Mrs Ayshford Sanford, owners of The Court from 1898 (insert). The Court today (right).

SHAKESPEARE COTTAGES, from their previous reputation called the Flea Bank and also known as the Pink Cottages and Bankside. These are some of the most illustrated and photographed cottages in England. Sixteenth century in origin, they were condemned in 1930 as unfit for human habitation but were restored and modernised by Bruce George during the last war.

Main photo: Shakespeare Cottages today.

Shakespeare Cottages circa 1910 (above left) and as depicted in an 1893 oil painting by William E Harris – but with artist's licence, placed in the lower High Street (above right).

Shakespeare Cottages shown on a postcard in 1905 (left) and with local inhabitants in 1886 (right).

TUDOR HOUSE
High Street

TUDOR HOUSE is a very splendid example of a 17th century house, with five storeys, fine chimneys, tall gables and mullioned windows. The bay window is unusual in Cotswold vernacular, the ball finials indicate a later date than the Lygon Arms. The dates 1659-1660 on the shield may indicate the date of its starting and its completion. In its time it has been an inn (The Angel), a school and a private house. Today it is the premises of H W Keil, one of England's greatest antique businesses. Starting as a cabinet maker, H W Keil came to Broadway as a salesman to work for Gordon Russell Ltd. In the depression of the 1930s he launched out on his own creating a firm of international fame.

The clock is known in the village as 'The Dummy' because it contains no machinery and is run from the adjacent building. It was erected in 1887 to commemorate Queen Victoria's Golden Jubilee.

Top left: The High Street in 1887, Queen Victoria's Jubilee. Broadway school children line up outside the village school. Above left: King Edward VII passes Tudor House in 1905. Tudor House in 1902 (left) and in the 1920s (right).

The building next door is now an extension of H W Keil's premises. It was built in 1774 by Lord Coventry as an inn called The Bell and Crown. In 1856 it was bought by a local charity and turned into the village school. In 1869 a further extension took place and the building took on its present Victorian neo-Gothic style with its little turret.

PRIOR'S MANSE
High Street

PRIOR'S MANSE *is very old, being built about 1320 by the Abbot of Pershore. The age of the building is suggested by the front door which is like the doors of early churches and quite different to the square ones of the seventeenth century, such as Little Gables.*

A drawing of 1820 (below) shows that the original building had a magnificent barn attached to the upper or east end of the building. This was ruthlessly removed in 1877 to make way for a dreadful Victorian shop (insert left). This in turn was taken down to allow widening of the road to Stratford.

LITTLE GABLES
High Street

LITTLE GABLES *circa 1900 (above). Notice the three doorways before its conversion, indicating that it was being used at the time as three cottages. Little Gables has just one front door today (left).*

COURT FARM
Upper High Street

Mary Anderson, about 1905.

COURT FARM was once the home of Mary Anderson (Madame de Navarro), the famous Edwardian actress, who died in 1949. In the 20th century this was the most noteworthy house in the village. Through its doors have passed kings and queens, prime ministers, musicians, and many well known members of the literary world. It was originally two farms, the upper farm being called Bell Farm and the lower called The Court Farm.

Main photo: Court Farm as it is today.

Left: An early photograph of Court Farm. The left-hand wing was originally Bell Farm which is particularly old and has internal evidence of a truck-framed mediaeval manor dating back to the 14th century.

Right: Court Farm in about 1900. The little boy is Toti de Navarro, Mary Anderson's son.

When the de Navarro family came to live at Court Farm in 1893, Miss Maud Valeric White, the well-known pianist and composer of songs, was living at Bell Farm. Eventually the family took over both farms and connected them by the addition of a splendid music room. Their gardens were designed by the painter and garden designer Alfred Parsons.

ORCHARD FARM
Upper High Street

ORCHARD FARM has the date 1626 at the front entrance and was once the home of Lady Maud Bowes-Lyon, the Queen Mother's aunt and the well-known politician, Sir Gerald Nabarro. The building in about 1890 (above) when Lady Maud and her mother, the Countess of Strathmore, bought the farmhouse in a poor condition and converted it into the lovely house we see today (left).

PEAR TREE HOUSE
Upper High Street

PEAR TREE HOUSE in 1885 (above) and today (left). This house was built sometime before 1772 by Sir Edward Winnington, Lord of the Manor of Broadway.

KEMPSON'S SHOP
Upper High Street

KEMPSON'S SHOP circa 1900, grocer, corn and flour dealer (above) and as it is today (right). Arnold's Shop next door is still run by the Arnold family today. At one time the Arnold's owned all three shops in the photograph.

OLD KEMP'S SHOP
High Street

OLD KEMP'S SHOP circa 1900 (above) and today (right). In the little lane to the side of Kemp's shop is a blocked-up archway. This used to be a blacksmith's shop where 'Old Kemp', a real village character (insert photo) fed his furnace and beat out horseshoes on his anvil.

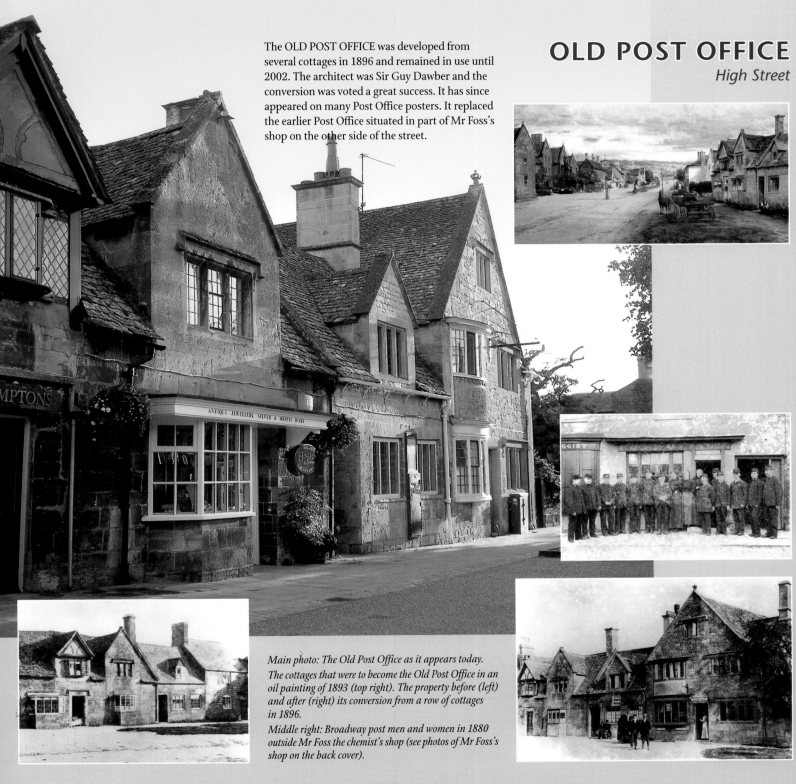

The OLD POST OFFICE was developed from several cottages in 1896 and remained in use until 2002. The architect was Sir Guy Dawber and the conversion was voted a great success. It has since appeared on many Post Office posters. It replaced the earlier Post Office situated in part of Mr Foss's shop on the other side of the street.

OLD POST OFFICE
High Street

Main photo: The Old Post Office as it appears today.
The cottages that were to become the Old Post Office in an oil painting of 1893 (top right). The property before (left) and after (right) its conversion from a row of cottages in 1896.
Middle right: Broadway post men and women in 1880 outside Mr Foss the chemist's shop (see photos of Mr Foss's shop on the back cover).

BROWN'S BAKERY
The Green

MR BROWN'S BAKERY and staff in 1924 (above) and as it is today (right).

BURROW'S SHOP
The Green

BURROW'S bakers and confectionery shop in circa 1900 (above) and as a modern art gallery today (right).